The Wonder of
BISON

For Matthew and Jenna, my brother's children.   — Todd Wilkinson

For Elizabeth Rose and Emily Louise, my ever-inquisitive daughters.
                                                    — Michael H. Francis

For a free color catalog describing Gareth Stevens' list of high-quality books and multimedia programs, call 1-800-542-2595 (USA) or 1-800-461-9120 (Canada). Gareth Stevens Publishing's Fax: (414) 225-0377. See our catalog, too, on the World Wide Web: http://gsinc.com

Library of Congress Cataloging-in-Publication Data

Ritchie, Rita.
    The wonder of bison / by Rita Ritchie and Todd Wilkinson ; photographs by Michael H. Francis ; illustrations by John F. McGee.
       p. cm. — (Animal wonders)
    "Based on . . . Bison magic for kids . . . by Todd Wilkinson"—T.p. verso.
    Includes index.
    Summary: Text and photographs introduce an animal of the Great Plains that gave the early Indians food, clothes, shelter, and tools.
    ISBN 0-8368-1558-0 (lib. bdg.)
    1. American bison—Juvenile literature. [1. Bison.] I. Wilkinson, Todd. II. Francis, Michael H. (Michael Harlowe), 1953- ill. III. McGee, John F., ill. IV. Wilkinson, Todd. Bison. V. Title. VI. Series.
QL737.U53R56   1996
599.73'58--dc20   96-5004

First published in North America in 1996 by
Gareth Stevens Publishing
1555 North RiverCenter Drive, Suite 201
Milwaukee, WI 53212 USA

This edition is based on the book *Bison Magic for Kids* © 1994 by Todd Wilkinson, first published in the United States in 1994 by NorthWord Press, Inc., Minocqua, Wisconsin, and published in a library edition by Gareth Stevens, Inc., in 1995. All photographs © 1994 by Michael H. Francis, with illustrations by John F. McGee. Additional end matter © 1996 by Gareth Stevens, Inc.

Printed in the United States of America

1 2 3 4 5 6 7 8 9 99 98 97 96

The Wonder of
BISON

by Rita Ritchie and Todd Wilkinson
Photographs by Michael H. Francis
Illustrations by John F. McGee

Gareth Stevens Publishing
MILWAUKEE

In western areas of the United States, you can hear bison galloping from far away. Their pounding hooves make a noise that travels through the ground. The noise sounds like a speeding train.

Bison live on the Great Plains, where the grass grows very tall. Bison eat the grass. Sagebrush shrubs and a few trees also grow on the Great Plains.

Early French explorers on the Great Plains thought bison were wild cows. They called them *les boeufs*, French words meaning "the beef." Another name for bison is *buffalo*.

In earlier times, millions of
bison roamed the Plains –
an incredible sight because
the bison is the biggest
mammal in North America.
For thousands of years,
American Indians lived on
the prairies with the bison.

People sing songs about buffalo. Cities are named after buffalo. Indians honor the rare white buffalo.

In the United States, there was once a nickel coin with a buffalo on it.

Bison freely roam Yellowstone National Park in Wyoming.

Bison ancestors were called wisent. They were huge animals with  horns 9 feet (2.7 meters) across! They lived in Europe and Asia.

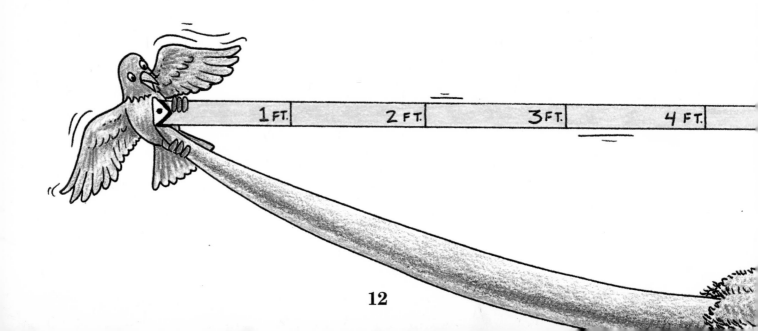

1 FT.   2 FT.   3 FT.   4 FT.

About four
hundred
years ago,
there were
sixty million
bison roaming

the prairies. American Indians
hunted the mighty herds.

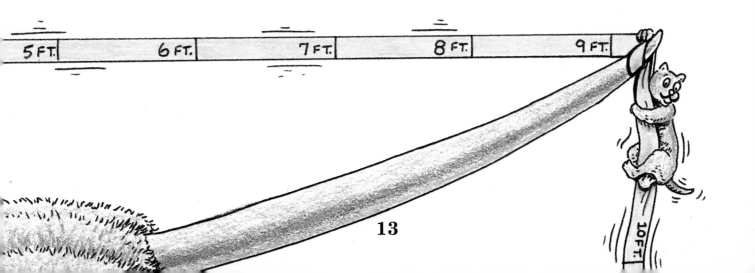

Ancient artists drew pictures of bison on cave walls. The first European settlers killed millions of bison for food, hides, and land for grazing cattle. By 1900, only a few hundred bison were left.

A male bison, called a bull, stands about 6 feet (1.8 m) high at the shoulder and weighs nearly 2,000 pounds (907 kilograms).

The hump on the bison's back is a muscle. It holds up the bison's large, heavy head. A coat of thick, rough fur covers the bison's body and face.

Cows (the females) and bulls have horns. Each animal has a beard on its chin and wide fur patches on its legs.

Bison enemies include bears, wolves, coyotes, mountain lions, and humans.

Each spring, a mother bison gives birth to a calf and nurses it.

When the calf is two years old, it leaves its mother. By age eight, the bison starts its own family.

In summer, bison fight for mates. Two bulls gallop toward each other. They crash their heads together and shove back and forth. The bull that wins this contest mates with a cow.

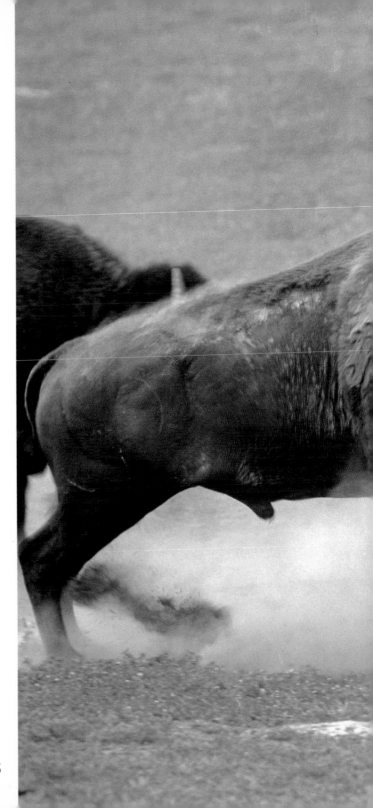

In fall, bison grow thick fur coats. Bison can stand the cold more than other Plains animals. They eat plants found under the snow.

People can observe herds of bison from a distance.

It is not
safe to get
too close
to bison.

When people or other animals get too close, a bison stomps or snorts or twirls its tail. A bull roars. A cow grunts. A calf bawls for its mother.

In summer, bison shed some of their fur. They swim or lie in the shade. They roll in the dust to get rid of bugs.

Bison move around in mornings and evenings.

Prairie dogs, mice, and gophers roam among the herd. They feel safe there from the hawks and owls above.

Prairie dogs dig tunnels where bison have trampled the soil. This helps grass grow.

Cowbirds
eat bugs
off bison.
Bison rub
on trees
to get rid
of bugs.

Bison are herbivores,
or plant-eaters.
A bison swallows
the plants whole
to fill its stomach.

Later, it brings
the plants
back up to its
mouth and
chews them.
This is known
as "chewing
the cud."

Bison waste helps the grass grow. American Indians and settlers burned bison waste as fuel for cooking and warmth.

Bison tracks look like this. Bison stay in herds for protection.

Bison are scared by thunder, grassfires, bears, and people. American Indians chased bison over cliffs, where they fell to their deaths.

Indians did not waste any of the animal. From bison, they got fuel, food, clothing, shelter, and tools.

Today, thousands of bison can be found in parks, zoos, and on ranches.

Glossary

bull – the male bison

calf – the offspring of bison

cow – the female bison

cud – food swallowed by an animal and then brought back up for chewing

Great Plains – the huge, level, nearly treeless region east of the Rocky Mountains and west of the Mississippi River

herbivore – a plant-eating animal

mammal – an animal that gives birth to live young that drink mother's milk

mating – the joining of a male and female animal to produce offspring

nurse – to feed young with milk from the mother's body

Index